Original title:
The Sweetness of Strawberries

Copyright © 2025 Creative Arts Management OÜ
All rights reserved.

Author: Elliot Harrison
ISBN HARDBACK: 978-1-80586-230-7
ISBN PAPERBACK: 978-1-80586-702-9

Sweetness on the Tongue

Juicy globes, so red and round,
They dance like clowns upon the ground.
A plump delight, I bite with glee,
Their laughter spills, it's all for me.

In silly hats, they roll and play,
As sticky juice just slips away.
A berry bash, let's not be shy,
Can't stop the giggles, oh my, my!

Petals and Fragrance

In gardens bright, they wear their crowns,
With leafy greens and snazzy gowns.
The petals blush, a flashy scene,
Like little actors on a screen.

Their fragrance whispers, 'Come take a taste,'
But watch your step, don't make haste!
A berry band, with jokes galore,
One slipped and rolled straight out the door!

Serenity in Red

In bowls of dreams, they pile up high,
A red parade that catches the eye.
But hold your fork, don't take a prize,
Or you might end up with jammed thighs!

They giggle softly when I munch,
With every bite, I smile at lunch.
A bursting pop, a juicy cheer,
These merry morsels bring us near!

The Berry's Secret

They whisper tales of summer fun,
Of picnics, laughter, everyone.
With tiny seeds, they plot and plan,
To take over the land, oh man!

Their secret's out, it's plain to see,
A berry banquet, wild and free.
So scoop a spoonful, don't delay,
Join the berry riot, come what may!

Warm Skies and Berries

Under warm skies, they shine so bright,
Little red gems, a delicious sight.
With each tiny bite, laughter will flow,
Juicy and sticky, oh what a show!

In the field we dance, a berry parade,
Chasing sweet critters, we're never afraid.
Filling our baskets, we giggle and play,
Watch out for the birds, they're coming our way!

Whimsical Red Treasures

Beneath the green leaves, secrets reside,
Whimsical treasures, we find with pride.
Wobbling like jelly on our grand spoons,
Munching and crunching under bright moons.

Giggles erupt with squishy delight,
Wiping our faces, what a messy sight!
Berry juice splatters, a colorful tease,
"Who knew fruit fights could be such a breeze?"

A Heart Full of Harvest

In the heart of the patch, joy is the goal,
With berry-filled visions, we're all on a roll.
Laughter erupts as we trip and we fall,
"Is it the berries, or me? Can't recall!"

Gathering wonders in our floppy hats,
Stashing them quickly from sneaky old rats.
'What a fine mess!' we squeal with delight,
A heart full of harvest on this berry night!

Luscious Crimson Whirl

Whirling in laughter, a berry cart spins,
Silly red globes give our faces wide grins.
A berry brigade, we march all in tune,
Dodging the sun while we dance under noon.

With each little nibble, we giggle and squeal,
Splatters of juice make for quite a meal.
Sticky and happy, we frolic and twirl,
Life's a grand adventure, all thanks to this whirl!

Savoring the Fruit of Forgotten Days

In a patch where time forgot,
Sun-kissed gems they grow a lot.
With sticky fingers, giggles soar,
A berry feast, who could want more?

Each fruit a burst, a tasty prank,
In my teeth, a juicy tank.
We make a mess, what a delight,
Wandering home as stars ignite.

Love Letters Written in Juicy Hues

A note penned with a berry quill,
Smashed smiles, what a perfect thrill.
The ink is red, the parchment sweet,
Come taste my love, it's quite a treat.

Each squished fruit tells tales of bliss,
With every bite, you can't resist.
A secret stash, our lovers' game,
Who knew fruit could cause such fame?

The Aroma of Sunlit Fields

In fields where mischief brews and bakes,
The air is thick with berry shakes.
We set a trap for birds in flight,
But only end up in a slice fight.

With laughter sweet, we slide and trip,
And claim the fruits without a whip.
Our noses stained with red delight,
We dance and sing till the night.

Echoes of Laughter in Berry-Picked Valleys

In valleys bright where we all roam,
We fill our baskets, bring them home.
With each round berry, woes take flight,
As laughter echoes, pure and light.

Slip on a berry, down I go,
Rolling in joy, what a show!
Chased by friends with berry stew,
Who knew such fun, from fruits we grew?

Ruby Treasures

In a patch where red gems hide,
Chubby critters take a ride,
Tasting fruit, they laugh and spree,
Berry juice drips down with glee.

Little hands reach for delight,
Munching munchkins, what a sight!
With faces smeared, they jump and play,
Oh, berry chaos rules the day!

Whispers of the Orchard

A sweet breeze carries tales around,
Of berry snacks that know no bound,
Giggling children run amok,
Sneaking fruit, what a plucky luck!

Silly hats and sticky hands,
Creating fun in berry lands,
With playful shouts and berry fights,
Who knew red gems could spark such bites?

Sweet Elysium

A berry festival, what a spree,
Dancing fruit, come waltz with me!
In berry hats, we twirl about,
With juicy laughs, we laugh and shout.

Sticky fingers, fruity hands,
A pesky bee, but who understands?
Chasing rivals down the lane,
Berry games, we are insane!

Morning Dew

Morning light and fresh dew drops,
Berry pickers hop and plop,
Giggles echo through the glade,
With every berry, a funny charade!

Laughter erupts as fruits collide,
In a battle of taste, we take our stride,
Juicy splats and all the fun,
Who's the messiest? Let's rerun!

Berry Bliss

In a world of red and green,
Berry lovers reign supreme,
Chasing flavors, oh what fun,
Who can catch the juicy one?

Squeaky shoes and berry stains,
Collecting fruit in silly gains,
With each bite, laughter rebounds,
In this berry bliss, joy surrounds!

Crimson Drops of Dewy Promise

In a garden so bright and bold,
Little red gems, tales untold.
Smiles sprout up with each small bite,
Nature's candy, pure delight.

With a squeeze, they burst out loud,
Juicy laughter in a crowd.
Sticky hands and joyful squeals,
A feast of fun, that's how it feels.

In salad bowls, they dance around,
Plopping down with merry sound.
A fruit that wears a silly crown,
Turning frowns completely upside down.

So grab a bunch, don't hesitate,
These delights will elevate.
Add some cream and take a trip,
On strawberry joy, let laughter sip.

Garden Songs of Berry Harvest

Underneath the sunny skies,
Little critters with berry eyes.
They nibble leaves, they plot and scheme,
Your berry patch, their wildest dream.

Baskets full, but watch out now,
The sneakiest birds, they take a bow.
While you search high, they dive for low,
A berry heist, quite the show!

Fields abound with frolic and glee,
Pies to bake, oh can't you see?
The laughter rises, pies do too,
Mix in some mischief, that's the cue.

So sing along, in berry style,
Harvest joy and celebrate a mile.
These tiny fruits bring such delight,
Turn dull days into pure insight.

Petal Kisses in the Golden Light

In fields of green, they wink and sway,
Petals soft as they start to play.
Bumblebees buzz, a funny tune,
Berries blush under the noon.

With each bite, a giggle spills,
Syrupy drips give summer thrills.
Fuzzy faces, smeared and wrong,
Bright red noses, we sing along.

Plant a patch, bring friends to cheer,
Berry bashes, oh so dear.
Hide and seek among the vines,
Each juicy catch, a laughter mines.

So gather round, share the fun,
With every scoop, we come undone.
From smoothies rich to cakes all bright,
In moments sweet, laughter ignites.

Heartfelt Moments on a Vaseline Sky

Clouds above, a slippery blue,
Below, red fruits with laughter too.
With each squish, a playful pop,
Giggles echo, we can't stop.

Silly ants march to the beat,
Fluffy noses, tiny feet.
Berry jam on toast, a spread,
Even the cat issued a thread.

Sticky fingers, faces smeared,
"Who's the messiest?" cheerfully sneered.
Chasing dreams, we tumble down,
In berry fields, we wear a crown.

So paint the day with fruity fun,
In this world, we're number one.
With hearts so full, we laugh and sigh,
Underneath this Vaseline sky.

Red Rubies on a Summer's Breeze

Tiny red orbs dangle with glee,
They wink in the sun, oh so free.
I reach for one, it hops away,
It seems even fruit loves to play.

In a basket, they gather with flair,
Each plump gem shines, beyond compare.
A mischievous bite leads to surprise,
Juice squirts out, oh my—what a prize!

Sweet Elixirs of Nature's Palette

In gardens where laughter grows tall,
A splash of red catches my call.
They giggle as I trip on a weed,
This berry's charm is hard to impede.

The jam I made, a sticky delight,
Splatters my shirt—oh what a sight!
Bread's never safe when they're around,
Each toast a chance for giggles unbound.

Tasting the Joy of the Orchard

Tiny treasures hide under leaves,
The aroma dances, and my heart thieves.
Each taste I take makes me grin wide,
These orbs of joy, oh how they slide!

Running through fields, it's a race,
With berry juice dribbling down my face.
The crunch and giggle, a combo divine,
Nature's candy, all yours and mine!

Whispers of Vine Underfoot

Beneath the vines, secrets await,
Little round wonders, oh what a fate.
One leaps up from the patch—but why?
Oh berry, you tricky little guy!

With sun-kissed skin, they laugh with flair,
It's hard to eat one without a pair.
A party of flavor bursts in delight,
With each crazy bite, it feels just right!

Crafted in Coral

In the garden, a fruit so bright,
Coral hues in morning light.
I tried one out, oh what a prize,
Juice ran down, I saw the flies!

With each bite, a giggle slips,
Stains on my shirt, I blame the chips.
Laughter echoes through the breeze,
As I'm dodging sticky bees!

A berry feast, oh what a show,
I wore a crown, made of dough!
A picnic gone, bursts of flair,
Who knew fruit could cause such care?

And now I dance, with berry stains,
In my shoes, the flavor reigns.
Crafted moments, oh so fond,
With coral fruit, of joy, I'm conned!

Garden Reveries

In a patch where berries lie,
I made a wish upon the sky.
A plump delight sat out of reach,
I leapt and tumbled, like a peach!

The garden gnomes began to cheer,
As I rolled like a ball of cheer.
Stuck in vines, I laughed out loud,
Hey look at me, I'm berry proud!

With each bite, my troubles fade,
In raspberry sauce, my plans are laid.
A splash of laughter in the sun,
Who knew that fruit could be such fun?

Now I sit, with berry dreams,
My shirt a canvas of bright creams.
Oh garden fairies, play along,
In nature's joke, we all belong!

Crimson Melodies

On a summer day, oh what a find,
Crimson jewels, oh how they bind.
With sugary smiles, we fill our pails,
   Only to leave behind the trails!

A berry tune we all must hum,
A sticky dance, oh here they come!
The squirrels join in our silly spree,
With tails a-twitch, they mimic me!

Tasting games beneath the sun,
Each berry bite is pure, sweet fun.
The laughter rolls like juicy tides,
   Capering skips and berry slides!

And now we boast of our fine haul,
With sticky hands, we've plucked them all.
Crimson melodies fill the air,
   In fruity chaos, we have flair!

Beneath the Berry Boughs

Beneath the boughs, I made my seat,
A berry patch, a summer treat.
The critters come to join the fun,
As I munch away beneath the sun!

A squishy foot lands on a berry,
Oh no, it's sticky! I'm feeling merry.
With giggles shared, we paint the ground,
Colorful chaos all around!

A contest now, who can eat more?
Juicy hordes, oh what a score!
Laughter dances on the breeze,
As we fight off playful bees!

The day rolls on with berry stains,
Brightly colored, ignoring pains.
We gather 'round with fruit-filled grins,
In berry bliss, the fun begins!

Nature's Candy

In the field where laughter grows,
Red jewels hide beneath the toes.
They bounce around, a playful sight,
Nature's candy, pure delight!

Frogs leap in, trying to pry,
Berry luscious—oh my, oh my!
They taste so good, they make you sing,
A fruity dance is what they bring!

Ants march in a goofy line,
Claiming these treasures, oh so fine.
Their tiny suits, all black and red,
Help them feast while others spread.

So grab a bowl, let's have a feast,
With giggles, silliness, to say the least.
Nature's sweet gems, a joyful trove,
In the berry patch, let's laugh and rove!

Berry-Magic Unfolds

Once upon a sunny day,
Berries popped to laugh and play.
They whispered secrets, oh so bright,
In whimsical shades of red and white.

With every pluck, a giggle shared,
A berry crown, who wouldn't be snared?
Even the birds joined in the fun,
A fruit fiesta, everyone!

So slip and slide on juice galore,
Rolling on the orchard floor.
With each berry squished, a silly sound,
Berry-magic spins all around!

When the sun dips low, who can say,
The sweetest tales of berry play?
With each bite, there's laughter spun,
A treasure trove of antics won!

Garden of Delights

In a garden where giggles bloom,
Berries giggle, dispelling gloom.
They bounce around, red and round,
Creating joy that knows no bound.

The bees partake in silly dances,
Buzzing to catch fruity glances.
Flowers cheer as they all play,
Join the fun; it's berry day!

Squirrels wear their berry hats,
Racing fast—oh look at that!
They grab their treats, then scurry and leap,
In this garden, the fun runs deep!

So tiptoe gently, giggle loud,
Join the fest, be berry proud.
In this garden of delight,
Savor laughter, joy takes flight!

Strawberry Kiss at Twilight

As twilight falls, the berries shine,
They flirt with frogs and laugh divine.
A strawberry kiss upon the breeze,
Wrapped in giggles among the trees.

Fireflies twinkle, dancing near,
The berries whisper, "Come and cheer!"
With every munch, a spark ignites,
Tickling taste buds and delighting sights.

The moon winks down, a cheeky grin,
As fruit lovers gather, let the fun begin!
With sticky hands and joyful shouts,
Berry laughter swirls about!

So come, dear friends, let's taste the night,
With berry wishes and pure delight.
This twilight kiss, a fruity thrill,
In every bite, a laughter spill!

Berry-Bound Joy Adrift in Time

A berry found on sandy shores,
Winks at me, it surely soars.
With a giggle, I take a dive,
This juicy boat, I must revive!

Sprinkled sugar on my hat,
I chase those posturing cats.
They dance away, oh so sly,
While I munch and ask them why!

Jellybeans in funny coats,
Ride along with silly boats.
A sea of red, they splash around,
As laughter trips on summer ground.

Time's a fruit that's gone too fast,
In this berry boat, I'll cast.
With strawberry sails, we shall fly,
Into the sunset, you and I.

Fragile Delicacies in Delighted Hands

In my hands, a berry bright,
Bouncing like it's full of light.
I take a nibble, what a tease,
It giggles back, oh yes, please!

Fragile treasures, do take care,
Slippery juice, oh, beware!
It drips and drops down my chin,
A happy mess, let's dive right in!

My friends all laugh, 'What a sight!'
Covered in red, I feel just right.
A berry bandage for my pride,
Oh, what fun on this wild ride!

Let's hold the feast without a thought,
For fleeting moments are never bought.
We'll giggle amidst this berry bliss,
In messy joy that we won't miss.

Sunkissed Beauty in Every Bite

Beneath the sun, they gleam and glow,
Dancing in the breeze, they steal the show.
I reach for one, it rolls away,
A berry chase to save the day!

With every nibble, sugar sings,
Oh, the joy that this fruit brings!
It clings to me like childhood dreams,
Unraveling in silly streams.

Caught in a cloud of sweet delight,
A berry fight ignites the night.
Squished red splatters make us laugh,
Who knew fruit could be such a gaffe?

In summer's arms, we twirl and spin,
This juicy game, we always win.
With every sunset, we rejoice,
A fruity giggle is our voice!

Sunripened Revelations

Beneath the sun, they plot and play,
With seeds of mischief on display.
A burst of joy with every chew,
Red raiders come for a berry stew.

The squirrels dance, the birds will cheer,
For these small gems that soon appear.
They laugh and giggle, share a treat,
While ants prepare their grand parade fleet.

Nature's candy, on the vine,
Wobbling like a wobbly dine.
Pick one and squirt it, what a mess!
A berry fight, oh, what a press!

With laughter ringing through the air,
Red treasure found without a care.
They slip and slide, oh what a scene,
In berry battles, love's routine.

Eden's Red Gifts

A garden dream, with a twist of fate,
Where juicy wonders sit and wait.
With every bite, a giggle spills,
Frolicking fruits that bring the thrills.

In rubber boots, we leap and dive,
Among the bushes, feel alive.
Jumping high, we pluck with glee,
Red treasure found beneath the tree.

Tangled laughter, a berry core,
A sticky mess, oh, what a score!
Purple stains and faces bright,
The kitchen's chaos, a pure delight.

With stolen bites and sneaky grins,
We munch away, our silly sins.
Eden's gifts, all ripe and red,
In fruity fun, our hearts are led.

Heart's Desire in every Bite

Red jewels glisten in the sun,
A berry quest, oh what a run!
With every chomp, a giggling fit,
Sticky fingers, can't ever quit.

In mischief's game, we take our stance,
In berry fields, we whirl and dance.
The taste of summer, sweet and bright,
Filling our hearts with pure delight.

Oh, the joy of a berry feast,
Where laughter reigns, and worries cease.
We trade our secrets, a berry code,
To share the love, and lighten the load.

With every bite, the world perturbs,
As giggles echo, and chaos swerves.
In nature's kitchen, pure delight,
The red, the joy, such happy bites.

Craving the Crimson

A little thief with a berry scheme,
Dashing through the patch, just like a dream.
With cheeks like roses, I run and race,
Hoping to find my berry place.

The sun sets low, the laughter rings,
Hoarding the treasure that summer brings.
We twirl and tumble, joy ignites,
See the warriors in berry fights.

With sticky hands and silly grins,
We chase the sun 'til twilight spins.
In every bite, the giggles flow,
As fruit-filled visions start to show.

Oh, crimson cravings, wild and free,
In every scoop, sweet jubilee.
With berry bliss, we find our tune,
Dancing beneath the laughing moon.

Juicy Red Bliss

In a patch where laughter grows,
Red gems hide beneath green bows.
They bounce with joy, the plump delight,
As critters plot a berry heist.

Oh, the squishy, mushy fate,
Of sticky fingers, how great!
With every bite, a giggle springs,
Nature's candy — oh, what joy it brings!

The crunch of leaves beneath our feet,
A frolic in the sun, oh sweet!
But watch your shirt, a dribble there,
A strawberry dab – fashion flair!

So dive into this fruity fun,
With red explosions, we have won!
Chasing giggles, taste buds sigh,
Life's silly, juicy pie up high!

Nectar of the Fields

In fields of red, where sunshine beams,
We squabble over berry dreams.
Juicy explosions, here they come!
Who knew red fruit could be so dumb?

Bugs laugh loud as we dive in,
Chasing sweetness, we won't win!
Each hop and skip, a berry flies,
In every bite, a feast of sighs.

A tasty prank, a berry fight,
Sticky hands, oh what a sight!
We roam the rows, a berry crew,
Complaining 'bout our berry glue.

So gather 'round and take a seat,
With goofy grins and dancing feet.
In fields of joy, we all unite,
For nectar's rich blend, oh, what a sight!

Sunlit Berries in Bloom

Beneath the sun, we laugh and play,
In cool shades of bright ballet.
Berries twirl like kids at cheer,
Nature's clowns, oh, they're sincere!

With hats adorned in berry crowns,
We strut and leap through grassy towns.
A splash of juice upon the nose,
Oh, such a mess, as giggles flow!

Then comes the bee, our silly foe,
Chasing us down, look at him go!
"Run for your lives!" we all exclaim,
While berries laugh at our wild game.

At day's bright end, we'll reminisce,
Of laughter sweet, and juicy bliss.
With petals soft and bright skies loom,
Forever captured, this berry bloom!

A Taste of Summer Dreams

A summer's eve and laughter reigns,
While searching for those juicy gains.
With every bush, a tale unfolds,
Of sticky fingers and daring bolds.

We race the clock, but oh! What fun,
Mischief calls — let's grab and run!
A berry bridge, we need to cross,
But watch your step, or you'll be the boss!

The ha-ha's echo through the field,
As sticky truths are revealed.
Each berry plucked, a treasure won,
And all together, we shall run.

So lift a toast to summer's cheer,
To fruity joys we hold so dear.
With bites of laughter, memories stream,
Oh, what a taste of summer dream!

Lush Red Lullabies

In fields of red they tease the bees,
With sticky fingers, we climb the trees.
Laughter bubbles in crooked rows,
While juice drips down like silly flows.

We squish them tight just to see,
If they'll bounce back like a rubber bee.
A splash of red on a shirt, oh dear!
"Fashionable" we say with a giggle and cheer!

Silly faces and messy grins,
Who knew this fruit would lead to wins?
We'll make a pie that's half a mess,
But oh, it's worth the glorious stress!

So raise a toast to our fruity plight,
A festival of fun, oh what a sight!
In each small bite, a chuckle gleams,
As laughter dances through our dreams.

Petals and Pips

A berry here, a berry there,
They roll away, I chase with flair.
Each plump bite bursts in delight,
Like fireworks on a summer night.

Juice like paint on a canvas bare,
I splatter red without a care.
My dog just stares, perplexed and round,
As I juggle pips on the ground.

Here comes mom with a frown and scoff,
"Why do you eat like a playful sloth?"
But I can't help it, they call my name,
As I dive into my berry game!

With petals tossed and laughter shared,
These fruity antics are highly prepared.
Let's eat and play, let's make a mess,
With jam-filled smiles, we call it success!

Charmed by Ruby Gems

Look at these gems in bowls aglow,
Can't resist, oh no, no, no!
I pop one in, like a pirate's treat,
Ahoy! A treasure that's hard to beat!

With every bite, my cheeks inflate,
A fruity feast that can't wait.
Like confetti at a surprise parade,
I giggle and squeal, let's notice the shade!

I twirl and swirl, a gummy dance,
In a hall of fruit, I take my chance.
To make a smoothie or two or three,
The blender sings the sweetest spree!

These ruby gems, so round and bright,
Turn any day into pure delight.
With each little pop, my worries depart,
For in this berry joy, there's a dance in my heart.

A Dance of Sweetness

Join me now in a berry jig,
With twirls and leaps, let's go big!
A taste explosion, such silly flair,
As we dance with fruit, without a care.

With noses full of fragrant bliss,
Oh, who could dare to resist this?
My friend trips on an errant berry,
We laugh till our sides feel very merry!

Let's wear a crown made of leafy greens,
And sing about our fruity dreams.
A burst of red, like giant balloons,
We'll raise our spoons and croon sweet tunes!

So gather round for this juicy spree,
Where laughter flows so happily.
Each little nibble, a twinkling delight,
In our dance of sweetness, we take flight!

Whispers of Crimson Fruit

Red jewels hang from leafy crowns,
Little nibblers dance in towns.
With smiles wide, they take a bite,
Juicy laughter fills the night.

Bright bows of red, like tiny hats,
Squeezed by hands of playful rats.
A splash of juice, oh what a sight,
Funny faces, each delight.

In nature's bowl, they're quite a stash,
Wobbling down, they make a splash.
But watch your step, my little friend,
For squishy spoils can swiftly end.

The garden giggles, ripe and sweet,
While giggling bugs complete the feat.
With every bite, the fun abounds,
In berry moments, joy surrounds.

The Juicy Kiss of Dawn

Morning greets with rosy cheer,
Tiny treasures reappear.
Little mouths that hoot and shout,
For these gems, no sign of doubt.

They bounce like balls on sunny trails,
Caught in nets and funny tales.
With sticky fingers, joy takes flight,
As laughter mingles in the light.

Ripe red wonders dance and roll,
Outrun squirrels—what a goal!
Chasing dreams of berry bliss,
Each moment's laughter—don't you miss?

Beneath the sun, they twirl and sway,
As happy critters join the play.
A juicy morsel, what a treat,
In every bite, life feels complete.

Orchard Serenade

Humming bugs in berry sprees,
Waltz among the swaying trees.
A plump parade of silly sights,
Strawberry giggles, pure delights.

In baskets bright, they take their flight,
Rolling down with all their might.
With faces smeared in berry bliss,
Oh, what fun, we can't miss this!

Friends and fam, they munch away,
What a feast! Hip-hip hooray!
With crunch and munch and silly sounds,
Laughter's echo all around.

In orchard blooms, a chirpy tune,
The fun continues, afternoon.
One last bite, they sing and sway,
As sunset smiles at the play.

Berry-Laden Promises

In fields aglow, the berries tease,
Wiggling joys upon the breeze.
With half a mind and sticky hands,
We dive into the berry lands.

Silly hats on silly heads,
Fruit-filled dreams spill from our beds.
A pluck, a munch, a giggle bursts,
In every taste, pure joy and thirst.

Tomfoolery in the leafy maze,
Finding treasures, lost in rays.
Watch your step, 'cause here they pop,
Juicy gems that make you hop!

With every berry, cheers resonate,
Laughter echoes, can't be late!
A promise made, oh what a thrill,
In berry dreams, the fun shall spill.

Lush Fields Under a Softening Sky

In fields of green where giggles play,
Fruity critters dance all day.
The sun shines bright on red delight,
As birds and bees take flight in sight.

A plump surprise in every bite,
Chasing sweetness feels just right.
With munching sounds that fill the air,
We nibble joy and shed a care.

Laughter rises with each spoon,
Thoughts of pie make us swoon.
Juicy jewels with laughter spread,
Who knew fruit could dance in bread?

So grab a bowl, come join the fun,
As fruity wars are now begun.
We'll feast on giggles, tart and sweet,
A berry party can't be beat!

Ripe Offerings at Dusk's Embrace

Sunset blooms in shades of red,
Nature's candy fills our spread.
The evening whispers tales so grand,
Of juicy treasures from the land.

We search beneath the leafy crowns,
For plump delights in grassy towns.
With sticky fingers and big wide grins,
Every berry is where the fun begins.

We try to share but end in fights,
As frosty daiquiris take flights.
The berry juice can stain our clothes,
Yet here we are, and nobody knows!

With laughter ringing, voices free,
This fruity feast's our jubilee.
So let's declare a berry cheer,
In dusk's embrace, we'll shed no fear!

Nectarine Dreams Wrapped in Green

In gardens lush where giggles sprout,
Dreamy visions flit about.
With baskets bright, we chase delight,
Each bite a thrill, our joy ignites.

Crimson globes hide in green veil,
As fruity treasure tells a tale.
We scamper forth with glee and shout,
For juicy morsels make us pout!

The ants parade with tiny feet,
As we steal berries for a treat.
With laughter loud, the harvest calls,
It's berry mayhem in these halls.

So gather close, dear friends of mine,
For every berry is divine.
We'll feast on giggles, no regrets,
In nectar dreams, let's have no bets!

A Dance of Scarlet and Dew

Awake, behold the morning's cheer,
With drops of dew and flavors near.
A berry ballet starts anew,
In fields where sunlight breaks on through.

We trip and tumble over vines,
Our laughter mixing with the pines.
Every fruit a wiggly tease,
In nature's party, we're the breeze.

With cheeks all stained in little splotches,
The fruity bits are now our watches.
Who needs a clock when joy exists,
In every bite of berry bliss?

So grab a friend, make laughter loud,
We'll be the berry-tasting crowd.
With juicy prizes, we'll proclaim,
This frolic is our berry fame!

Nature's Ruby Relic

Tiny gems hang low and bright,
Winking at me in daylight.
Redlicious mischief in a bowl,
A berry thief's delightful goal.

Squished between my fingers' plea,
Oh, how you giggle, mocking me!
With every bite, my cheeks inflate,
Nature's treasures, oh, what a fate!

Juice dribbles down my chin's side,
A crimson river, a sweet, wild ride.
Laughter echoes in the air,
As tartness dances without a care.

So here's to the berry, a cheeky tease,
A playful snack that aims to please.
In funny moments, you take the lead,
Nature's ruby relic, indeed!

Ephemeral Bliss

Oh, juicy globes of crimson hue,
Wobbling like a jelly, too!
A splash of laughter with every bite,
Moments cherished, oh what a sight!

One day ripe, the next a mush,
Eating them quick, there's no time to hush.
A battle waged with sticky hands,
A fruity frenzy that never stands!

Silly faces as I sneak,
My berry treasure, oh so sleek.
With a grin, I take a chance,
These fleeting treats invite a dance!

So let us feast, let giggles fly,
With pinky promises on the sly.
Ephemeral joys, let's not dismiss,
Each bite a laugh, a fruity bliss!

Forbidden Fruit of Eden

Beneath the leaves, they catch my eye,
A siren's call—a berry pie!
Plump and rosy, they wink and tease,
Temptation grows like summer breeze.

Oh, I know the tales so well,
Yet here I am, under this spell.
With fruity giggles and playful grins,
A daring bite where mischief begins!

They say I'm foolish for this quest,
But better berries are not like the rest.
With laughter bubbling, I take the plunge,
Each nibble's worth a cheeky lunge!

So what if they're deemed a sin?
In joy, I find my sharpest grin.
A fruit of jest, not meant to pout,
In this Eden, there's no doubt!

Fields of Flavor

In fields of red, I prance and play,
Where tiny berries laugh all day.
Their ruby coats, a cheeky sight,
Calling me to munch and bite!

With every squish and juicy pop,
I giggle loud, I just can't stop!
A berry battle with my friends,
Juicy warfare, where laughter bends!

A race to pluck, a bomb of taste,
Who knew fruit could go to waste?
With sticky cheeks and brightened eyes,
In fields of flavor, joy does rise!

So gather round, let fun commence,
For in this patch, it's all intense!
With laughter ringing through the air,
Fields of flavor, we don't a care!

Harvest Moon and Berries

Under the harvest moon's bright glow,
Berries giggle, putting on a show.
With little hats and shoes so neat,
They dance around, oh what a treat!

The neighbors peek and try to see,
What fun awaits, oh let it be!
A berry band with tunes so spry,
They twirl and tumble, oh my, oh my!

In the basket, a berry's plight,
'Hey! Let me out! It's way too tight!'
While one takes charge, a berry queen,
Says, 'We're the best that you've ever seen!'

So when the moon glows on a night,
Remember berries' dance is quite a sight!
A jolly feast in farmer's delight,
With laughter echoing in delight!

Red Velvet Dreamscape

In a dreamlike haze of crimson brine,
Berries bounce and leap, feeling fine.
They wear their crowns, all plump and round,
Shouting, 'We're the best treat in town!'

With whipped cream clouds and sugar flurries,
They slide down hills of strawberry worries.
'Watch out for the pie!' one berry cried,
As they dodged the crust, all lined and fried!

Frolicking beneath cupcake trees,
They hold a party, laughing in the breeze.
One berry asked, 'What's red and sweet?'
'This scrumptious world, the ultimate feat!'

A rubber duck joins in the fun,
Quacking loudly, 'Let's all run!'
The red velvet sky starts to shimmer,
In this berry dream, we all want to linger!

Taste of Siren's Summer

Siren's laugh echoes by the shore,
Berries plotting, wanting more!
They wear shell hats, so chic, so bright,
'Come share our joy!' is their delight.

The waves dance in a fruity splash,
While berries host a colorful bash.
With jellyfish in tangerine ties,
They put on shows that win the prize!

'Is there more cake?' a berry squealed,
While another rolled, their fate concealed.
Together they sang a curious tune,
Underneath a giant marshmallow moon!

In a sea of laughter, they swim and glide,
Adventurous berries, nothing to hide.
So taste the sun, let laughter beam,
With sirens and berries, life's a dream!

Sun-soaked Ecstasy

Beneath the sun in fields so wide,
A berry brigade takes a joyous ride.
With jaws wide open, the giggles flow,
As they feast on sunshine, a berry show!

In overalls, they stomp and play,
On ice cream clouds, oh what a day!
One berry slipped, took a dive,
'Help! Sweet heaven, come revive!'

As bumblebees buzz a happy beat,
A berry tells jokes, oh what a treat!
'Why did the fruit turn red in glee?
Because it saw the salad, you see!'

With laughter sparkling like so much dew,
Together they sing, 'We'll eat, me and you!'
In sun-soaked joy, without a care,
The berry gang dances, everywhere!

Nature's Candy Wrapped in Green

Plucked from vines, they gleam so bright,
A pop of joy, a pure delight.
Squirrels chuckle, birds take flight,
While tiny ants hold their own bite.

With sugar sprinkled, it's quite a sight,
Lost in a world of red and white.
Giggles erupt, it feels just right,
As hands dive deep in a berry fight.

Juicy Revelations in the Heat

Sun-kissed gems, oh what a tease,
Juicy dribbles, we eat with ease.
Faces messy, sticky knees,
Nature's candy brings such glee.

With every bite, a silly grin,
Today's feast, oh let's begin!
A fruity splash, it's messy sin,
In berry bliss, we all just win!

Rhythms of Nature's Red Symphony

Bouncing berries serenade,
As giggles bubble, smiles cascades.
In tangled patches, we invade,
A fruity dance that will not fade.

Cheeks are flushed, and laughter swells,
As we discover sweetened spells.
Juices burst like musical bells,
In every bite, a story dwells.

Stemmed Memories Resting on the Lips

Under sunbeams, we take a chance,
Plucking fruit in a jovial dance.
Tickled toes in nature's pants,
While flavors burst, we laugh, we prance.

With every nibble, a burst of cheer,
Savoring moments held so dear.
Stained fingers, we conquer fear,
In stemmed memories, joy draws near.

Echoes of Berry Delights

Red and round, they roll around,
In the basket, they can be found.
A squashy squabble, oh what a sight,
Who knew they could give such delight?

Squirrels plotting, they scheme and dance,
Hoping for a berry chance.
One little nibble, then it's a bite,
Turns a quiet day into pure delight!

With whipped cream hats and sugar suits,
Berry bands in berry boots.
Strawberry jam on everything,
Is this what heaven's like in spring?

Oh, how they bounce and how they jig,
Tiny fruits do a strawberry gig!
Forget your worries, take a chance,
Join the berry party, let's all dance!

To Taste the Sun

Juicy spheres of ruby red,
With each little bite, I see stars ahead.
Hand on my belly, oh what a thrill,
I didn't mean to eat my fill!

Run through fields where they shine bright,
Chasing shadows, feeling light.
Pick a few and drop a few,
Laughter echoes with morning dew.

Sticky fingers, laughter loud,
Capped with a hat, feeling proud.
Each pop of flavor, a giggle or two,
Mom's napkin's lost; who needs a cue?

Under the sun, we sing and play,
Chomping berries the fun way!
Taste the rays, soak the light,
In the berry bliss, we reunite!

Scarlet Hues of Happiness

Dancing on tongues, oh what a tease,
They wiggle and laugh like little bees.
Strawberry smiles, in every bite,
Squeezed out giggles, what a sight!

Pies in the oven, nearly done,
Flavors swirl, it's almost fun.
Mischief managed with every slice,
One more piece? Yes, that sounds nice!

Now they tumble, rolling away,
Stop that berry, don't runaway!
A tug of war with fruit in hand,
Who knew nature had such a plan?

Laughter blends in with the cream,
Makes me giggle, oh what a dream.
In shades of scarlet, joy abounds,
In berry bursts, happiness sounds!

A Poem for Summer's Fruit

Summer whispers, tastes abound,
Tiny wonders all around.
Spilling sunbeams, they bounce and play,
In fruity fun, we spend the day.

Strawberry courts, a fancy dance,
With every slice, they take the chance.
To flirt with cream, to dip and spin,
Winning the hearts of kiddos and kin.

Checkered blankets, sun shining bright,
Berry tarts in a friendly fight.
Laughter echoes, whoosh and cheer,
Sweet red wonders, summer is here!

Licking fingers, that's the rule,
As bridges of sweetness, we're all a fool.
A bite of sunshine, giggles surprise,
Enchanting stories, strawberry skies!

Crimson Delights in the Morning Sun

Red jewels peep from leafy crowns,
They mock my diet with sly frowns.
Chasing squirrels, I trip and fall,
A berry feast, oh what a brawl!

Morning dew and sticky fingers,
A jam jar smiles and sweetly lingers.
I plop and munch, a blissful sight,
Then stammer up, 'Did I eat right?'

Each berry burst sends giggles flying,
My breakfast plans? They are all dying.
With every bite, the sun starts to beam,
Oops, I forgot — I'm on a dream!

Friends join in with laughter loud,
Splat! One's face is berry-clouded.
We roll and play, oh what a spree,
Sticky fingers? It's the life for me!

Whispered Juices of Summer's Kiss

A little red orb dances with glee,
'Txt me!' it says, with zestful plea.
We giggle at lunch, who'll take a bite?
But oh, who knew they'd start a fight?

Splatt! A rogue berry flies in the air,
Lands on the cat — oh, what a scare!
Her tail twitches, her eyes go wide,
This berry drama, who can hide?

Lips are stained, oh what a sight,
Like clowns we look, but it feels just right.
We toast with juice, let laughter reign,
Best summer days, free of any pain!

With sticky hands and belly laughs,
We dance around, create our paths.
Summer whispers, 'Eat till you drop!',
As juicy goodness just won't stop!

Berry Bliss Beneath the Bloom

Under blooms, the berries sway,
Nature's candy on display.
I'm caught in thought, then guess what?
In my mouth, they hit the spot!

A berry lands, I chase it round,
It rolls away, on the ground.
That's how I met my berry friend,
Together we'll munch, it's a perfect blend!

Mismatched socks and muddy shoes,
Running wild, a game we choose.
Chortles echo, as juices spill,
On this journey, we feel the thrill!

With every bite, a burst of cheer,
Who needs salads, when this is near?
As giggles bloom, and laughter's near,
Our silly moments, I hold dear!

Harvesting Dreams in a Garden of Red

With baskets full, we make a stand,
Harvest time – it's berry planned!
'A little taste?' I make a plea,
They roll their eyes, but set me free.

In shadows cast by leafy green,
Out in the sun, I'm a berry queen!
Juices splatter, laughter flies,
Outrageous stains become our prize!

Each handful winks, it knows the joke,
Around the patch, we prance and poke.
Lush delights cheer our every bite,
And all our cares fade into night!

A prank or two? Oh what the heck!
With sticky hands, our day's a wreck.
In fields of red, we'll make our bets,
On berries sweet and silly quests!

Raspberry Dreams

In a patch so bright and bold,
Raspberries dance, tales unfold.
They wear their hats of sunny hue,
And giggle when they meet the dew.

Plump and round, a berry ball,
They bounce and roll, have a ball.
One snuck into my lunch today,
I swear it winked and ran away!

Juicy treats on sticky fingers,
Sticky notes of laughs it lingers.
I thought I'd share, but they conspired,
Leaving me alone, so wired!

Now I plot with berry dreams,
Finding schemes under moonbeams.
Next time, I'll wear a berry hat,
And catch the bunch before they scat!

Kiss of the Harvest

Oh, gather round, it's harvest time,
With fruity fun, it's simply prime.
The crops are ripe, oh what a sight,
They giggle in the morning light.

A berry kiss, oh, what delight,
I took a bite—what a funny fright!
It squirted juice, a splashy spray,
And turned my shirt to a shade of clay!

With every nibble, there comes a grin,
Like gummy bears dancing within.
These little jewels, what a riot,
Sweet shenanigans, oh, what a diet!

So let us feast, they can't resist,
Join in the fun, make it a twist.
With every laugh, and every cheer,
Let's kiss the harvest, oh so dear!

Drenched in Red Delight

In fields so vast, a burst of red,
Berry dreams dance in my head.
I pluck one near, it gives a squeal,
A funny friend, it's quite the deal!

With fingers sticky, I dive right in,
A berry battle, let's begin!
They rival pies with every splash,
I'm on a fruity, silly dash!

A sea of red, a juice tide flows,
With every dip, I giggle—who knows?
Caught in a tangle of fruit and fun,
These merry bites weigh a ton!

So here's to joy, in berry form,
With frolicsome fun, it's the norm.
Drenched in laughter, oh what a sight,
Berry feasts make everything right!

A Symphony of Tastes

When twilight falls, the berries sing,
A symphony of laughs they bring.
With every bite, a note is played,
In fruity rhythms, the dreams cascade.

From berry choirs to juicy bands,
In my mouth, a concert stands.
With every crunch, a thousand cheers,
Berry melodies through the years.

A brass section made of squishy sights,
With every nibble, a dance ignites.
Berries tumble, twirl, and sway,
In a funny jam, they steal the day!

So let us play this fruity tune,
Under the watchful, chuckling moon.
In every flavor, joy embraces,
A symphony of silly faces!

Scarlet Treasures on a Springtime Day

Red crowns upon green lands,
Nature's candy in our hands.
Scooping up with giggles bright,
Juicy plops—a silly sight!

Bouncy berries dance and roll,
Chasing laughter, that's the goal.
We giggle as they squirt and squish,
A fruity, crazy, splattery wish!

With every bite, a burst of cheer,
Sticky fingers, never fear!
Nature's pranksters, ripe and bold,
Who knew joy could come in gold?

A picnic feast, oh what a score,
On grass we tumble, wanting more.
Forget the plates, it's out of hand,
Strawberry warriors, let's take a stand!

Radiant Gems of the Earth's Embrace

Flaunting red with rhymes so sweet,
Nature's jewels that can't be beat.
Splatters on our shirts, oh dear,
Each juicy bite brings hearty cheer!

Twirling 'round, we gather fast,
Oh, what fun to make it last!
Chasing trails of sticky bliss,
How did we end up like this?

Juggling fruit like clumsy pros,
A berry showdown as it goes.
They bounce and roll, the game begins,
May the best muncher get dessert wins!

With laughter loud and cheeks a-glow,
The silliness begins to grow.
Hats adorned with fruity flair,
What a sight, we make quite the pair!

A Serenade of Juicy Euphoria

Oh, the giggles, bursts of red,
Splashes of joy where we tread.
Nature's laughter fills the air,
With every squirt, we do declare!

Hopping, skipping to the patch,
Can't resist the fruity match.
A sticky treat upon our face,
Who needs forks in this sweet race?

Gather 'round, the berry song,
Each plump bite sings along.
Dancing wildly, fruits collide,
A sweetened mess we cannot hide!

As laughter rolls like little waves,
We savor all the joy it saves.
Cherry red and bursting dreams,
Not one cares for the sticky streams!

The Taste of Sun-Kissed Bliss

Shining gems in clumps and curls,
Nature's giggle, sweet pearls unfurled.
Jumping in with arms spread wide,
Berry madness, slide down the ride!

Splat! A berry just took flight,
Dancing wildly, what a sight!
Squirting juice like little pies,
We burst into laughter, oh my, oh my!

Giggling 'til the sun dips low,
Sticky hands put on quite a show.
Tasting joy, it's quite a deal,
Oh, how silly this all feels!

Beneath the sun, we munch and play,
Making memories in this array.
With berry juice dripping down to our shoes,
We proclaim our love for this hilarious muse!

Harvesting Joy

In fields of green, we skip with glee,
Our buckets bounce, as we all agree.
Berries pop like laughter in the sun,
Each juicy bite is pure, silly fun.

A berry here, a berry there,
Wearing juice like strawberry flair.
We squish them all, oh what a sight,
Dancing around, feeling just right.

Our hands are red, and so are our cheeks,
We're berry bandits, so fun it peaks.
Squeezing fruit till it's dripping wet,
Laughter echoes, a joyful duet.

Scarlet Delights

In a patch of red, we pluck with delight,
Each berry shines, oh what a sight!
We munch and giggle, a sticky crew,
The taste is magic, it's berry brand new.

Chasing after bugs, we run and slip,
A berry caught on Mike's shirt, a drip!
We laugh so hard, it's a sweet charm,
With every bite, we forget our qualm.

We wear our treasure, juice drips down,
A berry crown, no need for a gown.
Tickly fingers, our faces glow,
Scarlet delights, the best show!

Fragrant Fields of Joy

In fragrant fields, the sun is bright,
We gather fruit till the day turns night.
With berry hats and boots askew,
Our laughter rings, a sweet, wild crew.

We spot a worm, and Max gives a squeal,
"Not a berry, just a big meal!"
With ninja moves, we dodge and dive,
A berry battle, oh how we thrive!

Sticky fingers, but hearts so clean,
Our berry feast, like a movie scene.
We scribble notes on napkins in haste,
"Best berry pickin'!" we joyfully paste.

Cradles of Flavor

In cradles of flavor, we find our fun,
Strawberry capers under the sun.
Squishing, crunching, oh what a sound,
Sticky giggles all around.

The dog joins in, he sniffs and sniffs,
Pawing at puddles, berry mishifts.
We caper over hills, berry pirates we are,
With jam for treasure, we've journeyed far!

Our faces sticky, like candy glue,
Every bite brings a funny view.
Amidst the laughter, we recall the tune,
Of merry berries beneath the moon.

Succulent Silhouettes

In the garden, they play hide and seek,
Juicy little nibbles, oh so unique.
Chasing after flavors, they make me grin,
One bite, and I'm hooked, can't help but win!

Red gems tease me from their leafy throne,
Nature's candy, but they're not alone.
With ants in a conga line, all hopping about,
Who knew picking fruit could lead to a shout?

I wear the stains, my fingers all painted,
Pillow fights with berries, I feel so tainted.
Bite into summer, squirt juice like a hose,
With every big splash, laughter just grows!

Giggles bounce like the seeds on the ground,
This berry fiasco is jesterly sound.
So grab your baskets, let's make quite the mess,
Strawberry laughter? Now that's pure success!

Sweetness on the Vine

Berries be bouncin' on their little stems,
Twirling around like they're dancing gems.
With raucous red cheeks, they chuckle and sway,
Who knew fruit could have this much play?

A fruit so small can create such a scene,
Slip on juice puddles, oh, you know what I mean!
Their laughter erupts at every mishap,
Like a slapstick comedy, on my lap!

Pick a few here, then trip over that vine,
My berry brigade is simply divine!
They giggle and tease while I tumble and fall,
With laughter so loud, I can hear it all!

So let's gather these jokesters, big and small,
With faces so ripe, they could really enthrall.
In this patch, we're royalty in berry attire,
Crowned in red laughter, oh, we never tire!

Symphony of Berry Hues

In berries' bright coats, a joyful display,
The orchestra plays; it's time to parlay.
With a strum of a vine and a pluck of a leaf,
These juicy musicians are beyond belief!

Watch them shimmy from sunlight to shade,
Making tunes as they sway in parade.
Lost in their rhythm, I can't help but laugh,
A berry fandango? What a fun gaffe!

Each morsel a note, sweet and impeccable,
Making my taste buds feel quite respectable.
Like a symphony seasoned with fresh summer zest,
These berry delights are simply the best!

Oh, the laughter we share, and the joy that we find,
In this berry ballet, no one's left behind.
With every sweet bite, let's raise our cheer high,
For laughter and berries will never run dry!

Sunkissed Nectar

Under the sun, they sit, a cheeky crew,
Cheering me on, 'Eat us! We're new!'
With sunburned tops, and smiles so wide,
These juicy clowns put my diet aside.

They bob and weave, calling me near,
"Don't be shy; have a taste, my dear!"
Sirens of sweetness, they beckon and shout,
Like tiny troubadours, they make me pout!

With laughter unfurling like petals in spring,
These juicy jesters make my heart sing.
So squish a few, burst of flavor and cheer,
And join in the fun, the laughter is here!

So come count the laughter and fill up my bowl,
In a frolicsome frenzy that fills up my soul.
With every sweet bite, the chuckles won't cease,
For in this berry world, we've found our peace!

www.ingramcontent.com/pod-product-compliance
Lightning Source LLC
Chambersburg PA
CBHW060130230426
43661CB00003B/374